My Best Friend Is Me!

By Beth Ann Marcozzi and Lawrence E. Shapiro, Ph.D.
Illustrated by Jille Mandel

Childswork/Childsplay, LLC
Plainview, New York

My Best Friend Is Me!

By Beth Ann Marcozzi and Lawrence E. Shapiro, Ph.D.
Illustrated by Jille Mandel
Designed by Charles Brenna

© 1995 Childswork/Childsplay, LLC
A Guidance Channel Company, 135 Dupont Street, Plainview, NY 11803
All rights reserved.
Printed in the United States of America

ISBN 1-882732-25-1

This product is published by Childswork/Childsplay, LLC. If any parts are missing of if you would like to receive a free catalog detailing other therapeutic games, toys and books, please call our Customer Service Department for assistance at 1-800-962-1141 or write to Childswork/Childsplay, LLC, 135 Dupont Street, Plainview, NY 11803.

Who is your best friend?

I have many friends. But sometimes they are all busy and I don't have anyone to play with.

So I make a drawing for my mom.

Or ride my bike.

Or read a book.

Or build things with my toys.

Sometimes older kids make fun of me because
I don't do things as well as they can. I don't like that.

But I know how to make myself feel better.
I practice things until I am *good* at them.

And I spend time with my real friends.

When I make mistakes. . . .

I know I have to try harder next time.

When I don't get an invitation to a party...

I have a party of my own!

When I don't succeed the first time,

I try . . .

and try . . .

and try . . .

until I get it right!

When someone tells me how nice I look . . .

I know why!

When I feel upset about something . . .

I tell people about it.

When I'm nervous or afraid...

I talk myself out of it.

When I look in the mirror, I like what I see.
My best friend is Me!

Draw a picture of yourself doing something
that is very hard for you to do.

Draw a picture of yourself in your best clothes.

Draw a picture of the person you admire most.

Draw a picture of yourself doing your favorite thing in the whole world.

Draw a 'First Prize' Medal. What did you win it for?

Ask your mom or dad if you can paste in a picture of
yourself when you first learned to walk.

What do you do when you are sad or unhappy?
Draw a picture of yourself doing something
that will make you feel better.

Draw a picture of yourself with a super-hero cape.
What are your Super Powers?

Draw a picture of everyone in your family.

Ask your mom or dad or grandma or grandpa to
draw a picture of when they were most proud of you.
Ask them to tell you about it.

Draw a picture of yourself helping someone else.
What are they saying to you?

**Draw a picture of your room.
What do you like about it?**

Draw a picture of yourself when you grow up.
What are you doing?